DC COMICS™ SUPER HEROES

THE SCIENCE BEHIND
BATMAN'S
GROUND VEHICLES

by
Tammy Enz

BATMAN created by
Bob Kane with Bill Finger

Curious Fox
a ...ompany-publishers for children

Published by Curious Fox, an imprint of Capstone Global Library Limited, 7 Pilgrim Street, London, EC4V 6LB –
Registered company number: 6695582

www.curious-fox.com

STAR37307

ISBN 978 1 78202 542 9
20 19 18 17 16
10 9 8 7 6 5 4 3 2 1

A CIP catalogue for this book is available from the British Library.

Editorial Credits
Christopher Harbo, editor; Hilary Wacholz, designer; Wanda Winch, media researcher;
Tori Abraham, production specialist

Artwork by Luciano Vecchio and Ethen Beavers

Photo Credits
Alamy: A.T. Willett, 12, ZUMA Press/Nancy Kaszerman, 15 (bottom); Courtesy of Boston Dynamics, 17; Defense Imagery Mgmt. Ops Center: Master Sgt. Jeremy Lock, 11; Newscom: Cal Sport Media/Paul Hebert, 16, Wenn.com/ZOB/CB2, 21, ZUMA Press/Sutton Motorsports, 9 (top), ZUMA PRESS/UPPA, 9 (b); Shutterstock: Jenoche, 7 (b); U.S. Air Force photo by Staff Sgt. Joseph Swafford Jr., 15 (t), U.S. Air Force photo by Staff Sgt. Bennie J. Davis III, 13 (left); U.S. Army photo by Spc. Kayla Benson, 19 (t); U.S. Secret Service, 19 (b); Wikimedia: BMK, 20, JFCAR, 7 (t)

Printed in China.

CONTENTS

INTRODUCTION

SUPER HERO WHEELS

Batman drives eye-popping ground vehicles. They range from the sporty Batmobile to the speedy Batcycle. Both are packed with powerful engines, bulletproof tyres and other amazing features. Best of all, many of these features exist in the real world.

CHAPTER 1
POWER BOOSTS

Batman's vehicles often use **turbochargers** to chase down super-villains in Gotham City. Turbochargers boost engines in our world too. These devices pump extra air and fuel into engines. They increase engine power by 30 to 40 per cent.

The BMW 328i sedan is powered by a turbocharged engine.

FACT

Turbochargers have boosted car engines for more than 50 years. The 1962 Oldsmobile Jetfire was one of the first to use one.

turbocharger system that forces air through an engine to make a vehicle go faster

ThrustSSC

Rockets give Batman's vehicles amazing bursts of speed. In our world, some **experimental** cars use rockets too. The Thrust Supersonic Car (SSC) uses two huge jet engines. In 1997 it set a world record when it reached 1,228 kilometres (763 miles) per hour. It broke the speed of sound.

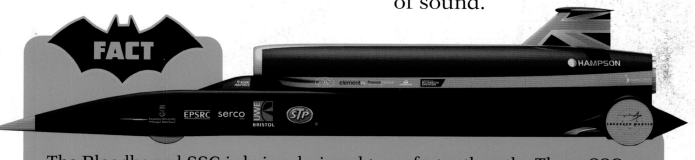

FACT

The Bloodhound SSC is being designed to go faster than the ThrustSSC. Builders hope to reach more than 1,600 kilometres (1,000 miles) per hour.

experimental something that hasn't been tested fully

9

CHAPTER 2
HIDDEN CAPABILITIES

Batman's vehicles enter **stealth** mode by
turning off lights and running quiet engines.

For the military, stealth aircraft can disappear from **radar**. A stealth aircraft's body is made with advanced materials and shapes. Its special design helps to absorb and deflect radar signals.

The F-22 Raptor's body shape and covering help it to stay hidden from radar.

stealth ability to move secretly

radar device that uses radio waves to track the location of objects

The Batmobile's ejection seat keeps Batman safe in a crash. In fighter jets, a pilot pulls a handle to use an ejection seat. Explosive bolts blast off the cockpit **canopy**. A rocket then launches the pilot's seat high above the plane. Finally, a parachute carries the pilot safely to the ground.

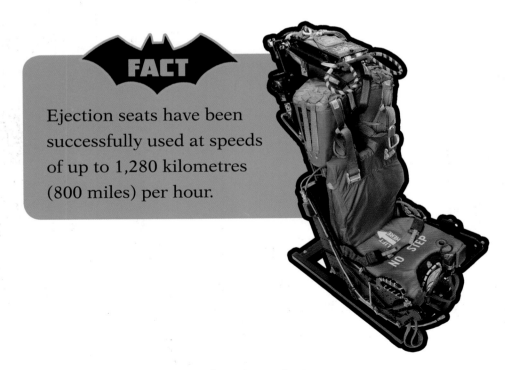

FACT

Ejection seats have been successfully used at speeds of up to 1,280 kilometres (800 miles) per hour.

canopy sliding cover over an aeroplane's cockpit

A pilot ejects from a fighter jet after guiding it safely away from an air show.

In the thick of the action, Batman's ground vehicles sometimes change into boats or planes. Some real vehicles do this too. The Gibbs Humdinga drives like a normal car on land. But in water its wheels fold up. Then, jets push it through the water at more than 48 kilometres (30 miles) per hour.

A Gibbs Humdinga glides across a marina.

The Terrafugia Transition is a flying car! It can be driven on land like a car. Then its wings unfold to take flight.

When bridges crumble, the Batmobile never fails to leap the gap. To get real cars to make these jumps usually involves a ramp. A ramp helps a car gain enough upward force to counteract **gravity**. In 2009, Travis Pastrana used a ramp to jump 82 metres (269 feet). It was the world's longest car jump.

Travis Pastrana flies through the air during his record-breaking jump in 2009.

A **piston** on the back of the SandFlea allows it to jump without a ramp. The robotic car can leap 9 m (30 ft) straight up into the air.

gravity force that pulls objects with mass together

piston part inside a machine that moves up and down

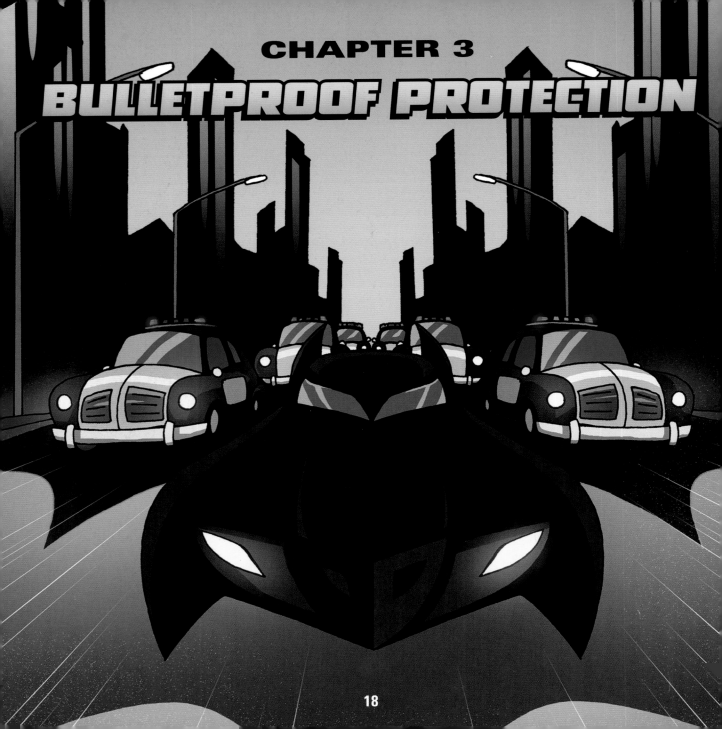

The Batmobile's body and windows deflect bullets. Many military vehicles have bulletproof windows too. These windows are made of a strong plastic sandwiched between ordinary glass. Bullets can break through the outer glass, but the plastic layer stops them.

A soldier peers through the bulletproof glass in an armoured Humvee gun turret.

FACT

The US president's car is nicknamed "The Beast". It may be the only car in the world with armour as strong as the Batmobile's.

The tyres on Batman's vehicles never go flat – even under gunfire. In the real world, **auxiliary** tyres keep many cars rolling along the road. These tyres have a solid inner ring. The ring carries the weight of the vehicle if the tyre bursts.

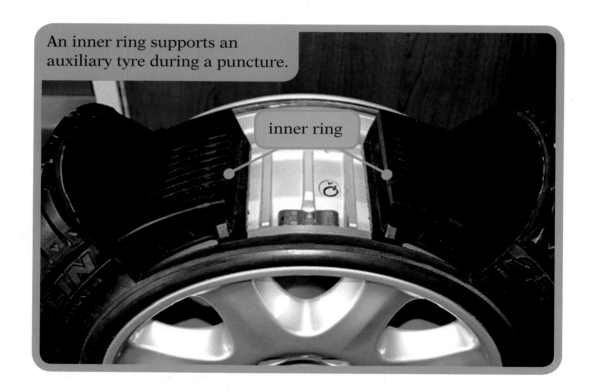

An inner ring supports an auxiliary tyre during a puncture.

inner ring

auxiliary helping, or giving extra support

FACT

Engineers have designed an airless tyre for the military. Its honeycombed pattern can withstand explosions.

Batman's vehicles rule the road with remarkable features. The real world science behind them is as amazing as the Dark Knight himself.

GLOSSARY

auxiliary helping, or giving extra support

canopy sliding cover over an aeroplane's cockpit

experimental something that hasn't been tested fully

gravity force that pulls objects with mass together

piston part inside a machine that moves up and down

radar device that uses radio waves to track the location of objects

stealth ability to move secretly

turbocharger system that forces air through an engine to make a vehicle go faster

READ MORE

Audacious Aviators: True Stories of Adventurers' Thrilling Flights (Ultimate Adventurers), Jen Green (Raintree, 2015)

Cars, Trains, Ships and Planes (Visual Encyclopedia), DK (Dorling Kindersley, 2015)

Great Car Designs (Iconic Designs), Richard Spilsbury (Raintree, 2015)

How to Draw Batman and His Friends and Foes (Drawing DC Super Heroes), Aaron Sautter (Raintree, 2015)

Incredible Car Stunts (Wild Stunts), Tyler Omoth (Raintree, 2015)

INDEX

READ THEM ALL!

THE SCIENCE BEHIND BATMAN'S UNIFORM

by Agnieszka Biskup

THE SCIENCE BEHIND BATMAN'S GROUND VEHICLES

by Tammy Enz

THE SCIENCE BEHIND BATMAN'S FLYING MACHINES

by Tammy Enz

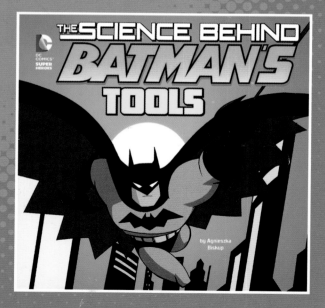

THE SCIENCE BEHIND BATMAN'S TOOLS

by Agnieszka Biskup